<u>GIFT</u>

Compliments of the Author

BEN FIELD

The Sculptured Courtesan

By

BEN FIELD

Author of: "Carcassonne," "El Camino Real," etc.

DORRANCE & COMPANY

Philadelphia

33670
PS
3500
F453S3

Dedicated to
ROWENA FIELD
MY WIFE

Acknowledgment is made to the following magazines and publications in which poems of this collection have been published:

Overland-Out West Magazine, Lyric West, Every Woman, Westward, Los Angeles Times and *Sunday Times Magazine, Los Angeles Saturday Night, Pegasus, Buccaneer, Circle, Lantern,* Edwin Markham's California Songs and Stories, Continental Anthologies, Christ In The Poetry of Today, *Literary California, Interludes, Silhouettes, Palms, Bookfellows, Adamant,* The Mitre Press Anthology, London, England, *Prism, Nebulae, London Poetry Review,* The Land of Gold (Tierra de Oro) Anthology, *Golden Stallion, Portland Oregonian,* Reason Magazine, Pacific Islands Magazine of Sydney, and other publications.

CONTENTS

POEMS OF SENTIMENT AND LIFE

CONTENTS

MYSTICAL AND PHILOSOPHICAL POEMS

CONTENTS

TRAVEL AND NATURE POEMS

FOREWORD

The tendency of the times is toward the demonstration of truth. And truth is being demonstrated by and through the psychic.

This Author, whose lines have caught the appreciative smiles of the people for many years now, in books of poems and on magazine pages, is a long-time adventurer on the road of the continuity of life.

He gives of his energy and consecration, in lecture, in creative writing and in service to the cause.

E. R. F.

July 27, 1935

POEMS OF SENTIMENT AND LIFE

Ben Field is one of the most popular lyrical and philosophical poets of the West. He is past president and one of the founders of the League of Western Writers; the Verse Writers' Club of Southern California; and the Masonic Library Association of Los Angeles.

Mr. Field is the author of three other books of poetry, Carcassonne East and West, published in 1932; El Camino Real; Poems, and Poems of the West, both published many years ago.

For four years past he has been the editor of Melody Lane page of poetry in *Overland-Out West Magazine*, the 66-year-old magazine of California, founded by Bret Harte in 1868.

A traveler to many far countries and leader in numerous literary and educational activities, he is engaged now also in lecturing, and in short story and prose creative writing.

THE SCULPTURED COURTESAN

The Courtesan,
to the Sculptor:

"Come close to me, boy—there's a bet
    On tonight. You are timid and slow!
  Come on with your red cigarette!
    My breath will keep it aglow.

"But your face, it is pale! Are you well?
    Are you ill or is feeling too strong?
  Press your cheek, sculptor boy, on the swell
    Of my bosom—I'll sing you a song.

"You're to carry me up where you sleep—
    In your arms—that's the bet, Michael boy!
  I won't be afraid nor yet weep;
    But I'll lie on your breast like a toy.

"The dancing's a dream, sculptor mine!
    Part the curtain that's hiding its charms!
  The Duke is out there with his wine—
    'Twas his bet, I'd not lie in your arms."

The Sculptor:

"If she hadn't hurt me to death!
    But she's mine! Do you hear me, great One?
Ah, I know that my joy and my breath
    Are forespent; but I'm here in the sun.

"And I swear by the bright light above me,
    I will do it, the stone cannot wait,
I'll carve her, an angel to love me!
    I'll make of her virgin, not mate!

"The sensuous grace of her limbs,
    Her intimate passion, her smile
Will be modeled to pæans and hymns—
    My chisel shall never defile!

"O woman, there is no debasement!
    We'll practice the magic of art!
Your statue shall stand on the casement,
    The glory of earth and my heart."

SCENE III—THE CAFE A YEAR LATER

The Duke:

"She! robbed of her beauty, the strumpet!
    And wants me to help—name of God!
She'll have to wait Gabriel's trumpet
    And find what's in store for a bawd!

"I owe her a something, she writes me,
    To brighten the misery I made—
Devil take her! It's ill she requites me—
    I'll not be bound to the jade!

"I'll ponder cool caution's insistence—
    A curse on the pity I feel!
'Twill be better to be at a distance
    When the cards are all dealt in this deal!"

SCENE IV—A GARDEN WITH STATUARY

The Courtesan:

"Ah, yes, good old watchman, I see!
    The statue is there in the light,
And he made it in glory of me
    Who won the Duke's bet, over night.

" 'Come on now,' you tell me, 'come near'?
    You're good to me, broken, forlorn;
O my heart, but his memory is dear!
    How I wish I had never been born!

"Ah, 'not touch it'? I'm reckless, you fear?
    But I thought, O I thought, yes, it seemed—
O Christ on the Cross, You must hear!
    He has chiselled my soul! I'm redeemed!"

TRYST OF YELLOW FIELDS

Fifty years, by the calendar, ago
   And spring was roistering, yet could not stay,
And we were truants in the morning glow;
   In the yellow fields we wandered away.

The downy cottontails scurried near
   And every mockingbird caroled long;
Over half a hundred years I can hear
   How the larks shot up with chrome-clear song.

There was Indian hunting and cowboy life
   And running away to the Spanish Main
And a boy's dream of a gypsy wife
   And gallant deeds that left no stain.

But now I am longing for that childhood crew,
   From my sumptuous room of lonely dower
And I passionately wish my playmates knew
   And could come to the tryst one quickening
      hour.

SAPPHO, ALONE

Sappho! Sleeping, still alone!
The moon and Pleiades have set;
Full half the lovely night has flown,
And thou,—and thou beyond regret.

Young time is passing, heart's one, now
Upon thy sweetly swelling breast,
And on thy beauty-sculptured brow
Should Phaon's head and kisses rest.

Sappho! Sleeping, still alone?
O wanton sweet, unknown to shame!
The recreant whom thy love hath known
Shall find nowhere a rapture's flame!

"OIL"

I hold it in a crystal glass
   Against the sparkling banquet-light,—
   Crude virgin fluid dark as night,
Caught in a globe of crystal glass;

For I must answer to the toast
   Of jade-black "Oil!" My glass is filled,
   While wine, red wine that once was spilled
On festive boards, is gone—a ghost.

I raise it high, the viscid oil!
   No Lethe slumbers in its draught;
   No zephyrs from Arcadia waft;
It visions blackened hands of toil.

But through the glass the light now shines!
   I catch the glint of molten gold,—
   The hues of caravans of old,
And ruby gleams from Eastern shrines!

I sense the God who understands
   The needs of peoples, as He smiles
   On valleys and unnumbered miles
Where He has hid the liquid sands.

Potential power for turning wheels!—
   To frustrate tyrants, set men free,
   Direct a nation's destiny,
Or drive strong ships with cleaving keels!

Raw energy to change the earth!—
   To bring bright gold to striving men,
   Surcease of work and grime, and then
Soft sighs, and love, and children's mirth!

I hold it in a crystal glass
   Against the sparkling banquet-light,
   Crude virgin fluid dark as night,
Enchaliced in a crystal glass!

LIFE'S GOLDEN THREAD

Life's golden thread throughout the ages runs.
  Sometimes its glittering presence men may see,
Like radiant beams from mist-enshrouded suns,
  That glint and flash, and leap forth daz-
      zlingly.

Ambition holds it on her outstretched hands;
  Vast empires weave it in their web of fate:
It binds the brow of beauty with its bands;
  It glows divinely in high deeds of state.

The sculptor follows it with carven lines;
  It makes the harpster's rhythms rich and
      strong;
Behold,—the painter's brush it intertwines,
  And with it, poets thread their sweetest song!

GYPSY LOVE

They buy and sell and barter,
   Back in the crowded street,
While you and I go wand'ring
   Where stream and forest meet,

Adown the poppied hillside,
   Out through some woodland door
Where ivy clasps the mistletoe
   On gnarled white sycamore.

You are a gypsy princess,
   I am your cavalier;
We do not buy nor barter—
   Save love for love, my dear.

GOOD-BY

Good-by! we lightly say it o'er,
  And when the friend has gone,
And we have shut the narrow door,
  Joy too is then withdrawn.

Alas! and did we know
  The turning of a street
Would bring us endless woe—
  That never again his feet

Would tread within our hall,
  Think you Convention's claim
Would put on Love a pall
  And let him go—the same?

Good-by! Oh, why did love of mine
  Not brush aside its fear,
My arms with eager strength entwine
  His neck in rapture dear?

Good-by! He thinks I love him not—
  He's far away amongst the years,
While life to me is ever fraught
  With pain and bitter tears.

GOOD-BY, MY BELOVED

I sit beside you and lift the white, cold cloth.
They spread it high above your head.
The flame is gone, yet is my love a moth
That can not still, though you are dead.

O tired unknowing lips and drooping mouth
That used to speak to me and sing!
O face that's silent as a weary drouth!
And hands how like a broken wing!

I drive them out, the hour and you are mine!
How oft have we communed like this!
Yet never again will I kneel at love's shrine,
While you have leaped the dark abyss.

Your heart is silent and your breast is cold,
There is no light upon your face—
I touch your hair reverently as of old,
The weavings of your bosom's lace.

FAREWELL

"Farewell!"
So Helen's song to Paris ran,
When the gates of Troy were battered down.
So sobbed an empress for the man
Who seized and wore a Frankish crown.
So Cleopatra to her king!
With passion's latest breath
She bared her heart to the poison-sting—
And looked aghast, on death.

"Farewell!"
A hurried word that blots a dream;
A blow from lips of coral-shell;
A smile that makes glad sunshine seem
Like cruel lightning out of Hell—
"Farewell!"

CHINESE SLIPPERS

Two yellow Chinese slippers on my table,
   Bedecked and filigreed with pink and gold—
I press them to my cheek, I am not able
   To put them on your feet as once of old.

Two slippers, almost new, but I remember
   When your dear feet were held within them,
      warm;
'Twas Spring-time of our love, now bleak
      December,
   And my regrets are as a winter's storm.

Two yellow Chinese slippers, in memory tapping
   As heart of yours was wont to do against my
      breast;
Naught could bind them to you, no silken
      strapping—
   Your tired feet outgoing at God's behest.

GUN LOVE

The fog climbs up the vagrant hills
   Like a roving, gipsy lad,
   And the little rabbits, cotton-clad,
Scurry and show their frills,
Like snow on window sills.

I come at dawn by trails grown old—
   Exulting is my heart—
   The soprano bullets do their part
From the slender gun I hold,
As they shriek like banshees bold.

The fog climbs up the slouching heights—
   I'm in Elysium then—
   What I did as boy I'll do again
For the joy of wild-land sights
And my gun and gray dawn-lights.

GUN BRIDE

My gun is a slender virgin girl
That I carry in my arms.
Over the hills where mad creeks whirl,
Alone, unwatched, I know her charms.
And she answers my heart's alarms.

I kiss her, my lips to cold, bare steel.
I strip her khaki cover.
Oh, the wine of life she makes me feel!
I cry with the oaths of the outland rover
When she stands with beauty bared to her lover.

What do I want with woman's love?
I have my loyal gun.
Let him who will ape the mourning dove,—
I caress, I kiss her, my intimate one,
Zestful of joy where the wild hills run.

FORGET-ME-NOT

Do you remember our tryst one day
   By the road from the little town?
We were two children out to play,
   While the westing sun went down.

The blossoming sage made incense hot,
   The purple laurel was sweet,
And a starry-eyed forget-me-not
   Were you as I lay at your feet.

Do you remember that hallowed spot?
   In my haunting thoughts it seemed
Just now a flame, my forget-me-not,
   Where we looked to the hills and dreamed.

I knew not the joy of the trysts we sought!
   The triumphs of passion and power
Are dust to the man whose heart has nought,
   But the innocence of that hour.

RETURNING

Love has come back to his old adventure
   With my wild heart, that once was a boy's,
With never a priest nor yet indenture,
   But only the welling of youth-time joys.

Love has come back with his old-time greeting,
   The honk of the wild geese over the fields,
A glimpse of a form, a wildwood, fleeting
   And I am one with the joy that yields.

Yes, Love has returned to his tragic hangar,
   The love of the sea, the farthest sky,
The hot sands' kiss on the desert; and a star
   Burns over the spot where Love and I lie.

THE SKYSCRAPER

When the last steel beam is finished
  And set in its lofty place,
When the last concrete is hardened,
  And bolted the final brace,

When slim and silvery upward
  The building lifts on high,
While its lace of architecture
  Delights the kindling eye—

When the rhythmic whole stands perfect,
  And the awed heart casts its guile,
As we read life's glorious purpose
  In that towering, God-like pile,

We will lift our soul's thanksgiving,
  Mounting it up to the sky,
For the proof that man can compass
  Whatever his bold hands try.

BALLADE OF A GOLDEN WEDDING

We joined our hearts, like clustered roses
    All abud in a fresh bouquet,
In a swirl of love as pure as the snow's is,
    We joined our hearts in life's young May.
    And 'twas fifty years ago today—
The maple trees their leaves were shedding,
    When we told our love in the old, old way,
And, O the bliss of our golden wedding!

Stand true! we cried. Till the last hour closes
    We will laugh and work and fondly pray,
Though life be strewn with thorns or posies,
    Our hearts shall cleave and never stray.
    After the toil came a roundelay,
And the way of love was fair with treading;
    The years that sped were blithely gay,
And, O the bliss of our golden wedding!

Look back, dear one, as time encloses
    This house of earth with a mist of grey;
Though the keeper rests and sometimes dozes,
    Love is as sweet as in youth's heyday.
    And still we are building our castles of clay,
That we take from the work we are never dread-
       ing;
    Like the poet's thoughts we steal away,
And, O the bliss of our golden wedding!

Envoy

Prince, we are crowned with laurel and bay
    As love's dear paths we are leally threading,
For joy has over our lives held sway,
    And, O the bliss of our golden wedding!

BALLADE OF THE GOLFERS' TEE

Hail, happy things that dwell
  In tropic lands or snow!
Hail songbirds with your spell,
  And gentle fawn and doe,
  And butterflies I know
    And mermaids of the sea;
  But when dawn comes aglow,
    Give me the Golfers' tee.

Hail men and maids, ah well,
  The wide world where you go,
In whom 'tis sweet to tell
  The joys of living flow;
  Old books I've loved to show,
    Old poems dear to me;
  But when dawn comes below,
    Give me the Golfers' tee.

O love in Asphodel,
  O passion's surge and throw,
O angel high from Hell
  Who gives me sweetest glow!
  O I my heart would row
    On river Life to thee;
  But when dawn comes aglow
    Give me the Golfers' tee.

Envoy

Prince, Passion is my foe,
   Love will not let me be;
So when dawn comes aglow,
   Give me the Golfers' tee.

SONNET TO A PAINTER

I've known a bud change to a perfect flower;
  A little bird outgrow its nesting place;
  A silkworm build its house of gauzy lace;
A boy become a man in one swift hour;
An artisan construct a work of power,
  A man invent an intricate machine,
  The earth produce a vine from out a bean,
And love grow strong without the thought of
    dower.
But yesterday I saw a woman paint,
  With pigments bright as earth beneath the sun.
  The magic of it I can never tell.
She wore the hallowed beauty of a saint,
  And when the brilliant canvas all was done,
  It proved the one transcendent miracle.

BEAUTY AND LOVE

Straight is the line of beauty,
Nor curved as often said.
Look far away over ocean,
Across the briny bed;

Straight is the long horizon,
Straight as the line of duty,—
Though heaven is arched above us,
Straight is the line of beauty.

Old ocean's bed is bended,
Old ocean's surface too;
But beauty is not ended
When straight it runs from you.

Straight is the line of beauty!
When love has made retreat
The heart has one sweet duty,
Straight to the loved one's feet.

COME BACK

Come back! just as you used to come
When first I saw your eyes
Peering at me shyly over the edge
Of love's battlement.

You were so fair and I so dumb,
But those dear California skies
Throbbed with the pulsing of our love
And all the flowers and buds
Breathed kisses that I sent.

Come back, come back,
My Southern tropic flower!
Come back and love me as you first were meant,
If not for aye, then come for one sweet hour.

THE BLIND LOVER

Earth knew him as her botanist,
  A king among the flowers;
Then o'er his eyes came blinding mist
  And darkened were his hours.

A pure and lovely girl was she,
  Inspired by joy and song,
With pity sweet for those in pain
  And tears for want and wrong.

One day, as was her habit kind,
  She brought in radiant bloom,
The fairest flowers that she could find
  To banish care and gloom.

The nurses white went to and fro,
  The matron's voice was kind:
"Here, child! with thy fair roses go
  To him whose eyes are blind,

"So shall the angels give thee pay
  For charity of thine,
Go! take to him this fair bouquet
  Of mystic flowers divine."

She entered then the darkened room,
With eager, hurrying feet;
A man arose within the gloom,
Oh, heavenly smile and sweet
That lit his face!
He seized the flowers!
With rapid pace
He reached the sash
And threw it wide!
The thing was rash,
But steady was his hand!
He saw! the light of day
Was in his eyes, the hours
That science took to cut and brand,
The weary length of night,
Were gone!
And here were flowers!
His flowers, his goal!
And dawn,
Fair dawn again of sight!
He faced the girl
And clasped her in his arms;
He kissed her till delight
Made radiant all her charms;
Then quick and glad
To see pure love light up his face,
She helped him place
The roses in the rays of light,
And murmured, to relieve her plight:
"God's love knows only perfect sight."

A BAUBLE ON A STRING

Wharto: "My Lord, the Princess found a
bauble on a string."
Lord: "Love's offering."
Wharto: "Her eyes, my Lord, were full of
tears."

Love laid an offering down—
It was the thing he had:
Other it could not be
Or it were not his.
Love picked the offering up,
But, hold! was it love, indeed,
That shone in her dark eyes
That time she stooped
And took the bauble in her hand?
Ah, well! we'll call it love.
As he remembers how she looked,
Those happy days,
He is ready now to swear
Her love was fairer even than his.
She held the bauble gift on high—
It was his love—
And in the crystal toy
Beheld a mirror of her moment's joy.

Remember, it was his gift—
The dearest thing he had,
Rang true of what he was,

Pretended not to be a gem
Of rarest worth;
But spoke of simple faith
And utter human liking.
Other toys he had,
Companionship and idle talk,
And hands that touched,
And studious hours together,
And walks where miles were minutes,
And trysts that made a palace
Of a hovel,
And shady, sylvan glen
Unknown to other men.

Thus time went by uncounted
And still she held the bauble in her hand.
She was as fair as life,
Her cheek a cameo, cut,
Her whole bright self
A sparkling gem
Whose myriad facets
Flashed all beauty forth,
All grace and charm the world had ever known.
And still she held his bauble in her hand,
And he is wont to say
Her love, in truth, the greater was.
And yet he loved—
It was what he had,
The bauble, all of glass,
God made him thus—alas!

Time's wheel turns on—
The alchemist makes gold,
The furnace heat returns a diamond,
Emotions, mingling, melt,
Ambition urges on accomplishment,
And hearts forget;
But one, a recluse in the haunts of men,
Ofttimes doth start with pain,
Remembering his Princess and her grace,
Remembering her eyes, her hair, her face.

One day when clouds were in the sky
And time had passed
And put its mark on men and things,
A lady, weary of her rest
And weary of her loneliness,
Ransacked her playthings
Of another day.
She found a bauble on a colored string
And held it in her hand.
"He called it love," she said;
"But, God! It was what he had,
A weak and foolish gift, perhaps,
Yet his, his and he gave it to me!
I wonder if his eyes can see,
Or if, like mine, they're dim with tears."

FOR PEACE

She kneels
With head thrown up to God
And arms stretched high.
Her bronze breast
Rests upon a blackened cannon.
Across the cannon
Sprawls the body of a youth—
Shot and shell have murdered him
And maimed his limbs.
Upon the face of her who supplicates
There is a horror,
A dumb pleading.

No flag, no sword,
No silent drum nor fife—
Only the agony of the world.

Written after seeing the bronze statuary, Altar
of Nations, by Ella Buchanan.

THE HOME I WORSHIPED IN

I've gently bade them all "good-by,"
  The homes I've lived within,
Sometimes, alas, with grief and sigh;
  Though often it has been
With just a comrade's "fare-you-well."
  Yet every last adieu
Has left the clinging, subtle spell
  Of joys I'd fain renew.

I've lowered the blinds and paced the floor
  And parted from a friend;
With thoughts of love I've closed the door.
  I've said "good-by"—God send
His strength to save, in memory's life,
  The joy that might have been—
A baby in the arms of wife—
  The home I worshiped in.

THE HARP

O harp of golden hue,
Come from a mystic land!
With reverent soul and hand
I try to seize and hold
Your singing tones of gold.
An angel's touch
Inspires your chords,
While yellow strands of hair
Commingle with your strings.

I heard you at a castle in Palestine.
Great Richard of the Lion Heart
Was there,
As Blondel caroled for the Christ
And touched you with a reverence divine.
The nightly wassail
Of the King
Could not prevail.
You made men sing
And made men pray:
You were a stronger armor
Than rich battle mail,
And I did love you
On that ancient day.

I saw you in the bright van
Of a host on high.
Down the lengthy span

Of Heaven you went by:
Archangels shouted in your tunes.
Hosannas like rich runes
Came back from where you led,
And all the winds accompanied.

O harp!
Instrument divine,
Wed to music, wed to wine,
Minstrel in the gardens of Proserpine!
You glorious, golden thing,
Tuned in the fields of asphodel
Of high, white God!
By all bright beings' joys
And all the loves in Paradise
Of angel girls and choir-sweet boys,
By all His lilied blossoming,
By all His holy spell
That overflows the courts of Heaven
And finds its silvery way,
Like star dust, to the lower sod—
I hail you,
Wing of God!

HEART-CONTENTMENT

Dear Christ, here is a smile for you,
  A smile for every day;
I walk the aisles of orange through,
  The golden leafy way.

How could I help but smile, dear God?
  In the land where men are free;
My arm has strained to turn the sod,
  To pluck the fruit from the tree.

Dear Christ, the westing sun is low,
  My humble lot is blest,
And I return with joy aglow
  To wife and home and rest.

ON CARING FOR HIS FIANCÉE'S WARDROBE OVERNIGHT

It's longing midnight in my room
And almost are you here,
A bride beside her longing groom,
A darling bride and dear.

For have I not your blush pink gown
And pink and perfumed hose,
And little powder puff of down
And on the gown a rose?

The dainty shoes that held your feet
I kiss, I kiss your lace,
And every thought's as pure and sweet
As your own angel face.

JACK-IN-THE-BOX

Oh, I am Jack-In-The-Box,
   With a part in the festal throng;
I have motley and paint that shocks,
   I've a love for wassail and song.

I'm up, I'm up in the box!
   I'm the Jack who livens the crowd!
Though you shut me with lid and with locks,
   I'm up again painted and proud.
Oh, I am Jack-In-The-Box!
   I laugh, and I laugh again loud.

I'm Jack-In-The-Box, am I,
   With never a soul nor a shroud;
I mock at the world, as I cry
   Folly and fun to the crowd.

Oh, never a soul have I!
   I'm a toy of bedizened wood;
My gestures are only a lie—
   I do as I'm told I should.

Yes, painted Jack-In-The-Box,
   Gay Jack-In-The-Box, am I.
My fun at your heart door knocks—
   See—I've made that fair lady cry.

But some day I think I'll awake
    With a soul, and a heart-beat, too,
For that little child with the cake—
    He believes my antics are true!

SILENT AT SIXTY

You say your lyric words lie dead
    Because your three score years have run,
Because your passion-time has fled,
    Youth's milk-white fairness turned to dun.

God's pity! Never did you know
    What songs they are the poets hear!
If you could sing them in your snow
    They'd melt and wash away your fear.

Song does not die nor sound less fair
    Because man's downy years have passed:
While genius breathes its Attic air
    This earthly love and youth shall last.

TWO SHELLS

I found two shells upon the beach,
Kathleen,
And harmonies of song
Came forth from each.
I cherished long
That treasure trove
Until my ship a-sail hove
Questingly in sight of land—
There walked a maid and youth with hand in
        hand,
The maid was you, the youth was I,
Love's old dear light was in the sky.
I pinned the shells upon your breast,
The rounded years know well the rest,
Kathleen.

TRUE TO ART

O one there came who thrilled my soul
At the banquet hall to-night!
Her face was framed in an aureole
Of hair that shimmered bright.

Her eyes were brave and unafraid,
Her smile was sweet as the dawn;
Ah, she was the wonderful Art-child maid—
Her voice like a silvered horn.

The sybarite, from his crippled birth,
And the gourmand came to dine,
And she who had sold for tinseled worth
God's raiment that is divine.

But the one with hair of aureole,
Looked on with a fearless heart,
And held her love and her woman's soul
True to the glory of Art.

SWEETHEART

Sweetheart, I sail away to thee
  Wherever the helmsman steers;
Wherever the main is wild and free
  My good hopes banish tears.

Sweetheart, I strive for none but thee,
  Wherever my swift feet tread;
What task my eager eyes may see,
  I do for hope ahead.

Sweetheart, of thee I dream, away,
  Or under home-starred skies;
Walking with thee my fond thoughts stay,
  Held by thy tender eyes.

Ah, true, I know thee not, Sweetheart!
  And yet, dream-kissed alone,
Of me thou still art very part—
  My soul's ideal—my own.

LYRICLAND

I lived in a happy lyricland
  And its horns blew sweetly to me,
In the rose of the early morning
  And the turquoise light of the sea.

I heard the silver bugles,
  I glimpsed another sphere
And gazed with adoration
  On poet and singer and seer.

O fairy elves of lyricland
  Your love and art shall chime,
While your piping horns of rapture
  Blow joy and song and rhyme.

TOUCH OF NATURE

There is a day of all days best
  When in a tree the summer long,
All builded fair their little nest,
  Birds fill the air with sweetest song.

Five eggs, like pearls in coronet,
  Lie there a hidden, beauty quest,
And on the eggs the bride doth set
  And watch the bridegroom's flashing vest.

There is a day of all days best
  When love between a girl and boy
Hath banished from the world the rest
  Of us and left them only joy.

There is a day of all days best
  When, fairest gift from Heaven above,
The rosy bride to mother's breast
  Holds fast a babe of dual love.

HEART OF HUNGER

Grey streaks her glorious crown of hair,
The years have put her hope to rout:
Did she accept this state as fair,
Or thrust on her with passion's drought?

One says she's glorified with joy,
Working to right all women's wrongs;
But see her kiss that baby boy
And tremble at his cradle songs!

UNFATHOMABLE

What is the goal,
Of this dream of Life?
Flesh fighting soul—
Like the call of a fife.
O spirit beware
Lest hearts shall fashion,
Out of loveliness there,
And the sinews of passion,
A temple too fair.

TO MY LADY

If ever I have hurt you
O Lady, who art my light,
If ever my selfish longing
Has put your trust to flight;

O Lady, My Lady, forgive me
If ever I lightly hold
The trust in your dear eyes shining—
That's priced above gems or gold.

THE SURE RETURN

She will return if treated fairly, rightly,
　　Though once her love was crucified,
Though she may laugh at protests lightly,
　　She will return, with you abide.

I have beheld the strong earth sleeping,
　　Crowned with glory in East and West,
And fickle ocean as a mistress from him creep-
　　　　ing,
　　But to return with passion to his breast.

So shall dear love come back to hearts with sor-
　　　　row welling,
　　If they will hold to ideals true,
Return and haunt again its ancient dwelling,
　　That was a fairy castle built perhaps by you.

PAGAN

All beauty's yours, all joy is yours,
All dearest longings right—
The Pagan gods kill who endures
To stand against their might.

Then take to self life's very best,
Seek time's quick, fleeting charms—
Worship the impassioned, willing breast
That's eager for your arms.

HOLD LOVE FOREVER FAIR

Beware how Love conducts himself!
What status shall he have with comradeship?
The filmy gauze that floats about the elf
Is crushed sometimes in passion's grip.

Renew Love's halo then,—
Reweave the gauzy lace
That was his dear delight when
First you knew him face to face.

LOVELESS THROUGH LIFE

Drab are the hues of her morning, straight-lined
    dress
    And lonely the unfrequented paths she treads;
Yet in her soul there is a surer guess
    Because she knows not perfumed marriage-
    beds.

Two goals there are, but one is nobly served,—
    Either warm love and motherhood are yours,
Or modest the maidenhood that has not swerved
    From chastity, nor turned to man's allures.

A truer guess than even motherhood's,
    Of how life builds on earth and disappears;
For spinsterhood there are some spirit moods
    That outshine love all down the changing
    years.

STRENGTH

To live, a man,
In all that manhood means,
To be a god on earth
And drink life's cup,
And conquer all the fates, and know
Dominion in my years.

TO A NEWSBOY

Ragged boy with wistful eyes,
　　Earning scanty dimes,
You often dream of summer skies
　　And dear vacation times.

Ragged boy with only part
　　Of boyish things to gladden,
Eyes of sorrow touch my heart,
　　Childish longings sadden.

Boy so young were hardly made
　　To battle with life's sorrows,
But with you I'd gladly trade
　　To have all your tomorrows.

Boy of street and alley breeding,
　　Life is all for you
As you wander, little heeding
　　What there is to do.

Ragged boy with wistful eyes,
　　Dreaming of your goal,
If you want a kingly prize—
　　Master your own soul.

OH, SAY, LITTLE BOY!

I'll sail away to lullaby land
Where my little boy goes when asleep,
Where cockle shells roll on the yellow sand,
And the water is only knee deep.

Along the shore of that shining strand
We'll meet where the breaker combs,
And you and I with hand in hand
Shall visit the little homes
Of the pretty people of poppy land,
Who receive on a drowsy day,
And the little brown maids with a brownie band
Shall sing in a wonderful way.
The trooping elves from the hills will come,
And the mermaids comb their hair,
While you and I with the wee ones roam.
Each star will have a stair
Stretching away over waters deep
And rising into the night,
Where the angels play,—nor once know sleep—
Bo-peep, until morning light.

Oh, say, little boy, will you meet me there?
And I will play with you—
Up and up the golden stair
We'll climb to Heaven's blue!

TONY AND HIS DOG

He lived at Sunnyside
Where city quiets toward the sea,
A man who'd traveled wide,
Then settled down like you or me.

He labored with his hands
And wheresoe'er he went about the wide estate
His dog went too, o'er new-plowed ground and
      fallow lands,
Each to the other, mate.

An hundred children loved this simple man,
His dog's devotion was a splendid thing,—
For trust of child and dog since time began
Has made the humble, rival of the king.

The other night he sat beside a rustic fence,
His long-used pipe within his hand,
And morning found him there, his spirit sum-
      moned thence
To that last bourne and promised land.

Thus Tony and his dog alone,
Side by side from accustomed, loving choice,
The one insensate as the stone,
The other whining for his master's voice.

MYSTICAL AND PHILOSOPHICAL
POEMS

THE RHYTHM OF LIFE

Mute and unshaped in marble hills
  Are unevoked Mercurys lying,
Fairer of form, with power more rife
  Than gladiators dying.

Has sculptor cut a Venus face
  Or shaped a warrior's bust?
The dream undreamed is fairer yet
  Than these that turn to dust.

Up where the air is ether
  Keen as the edge of a knife,
Down deep in the heart of nature—
  The bright rhythm of Life.

THE SIGN OF THE ULTIMATE

I stood on an island sea beach.
No other soul was there
Save the soul of the island sleeping
And the soul of God in the air.

The beach was long and lonely;
And my soul was lonely too.
No being gave me greeting,
Tho above the sea-birds flew.

Full well I knew the sea of life,
Full long I'd searched its deeps;—
But now, behold, oncoming,
A wave that landward sweeps!

I see with eyes far seeing,
And know with thought profound.
I hear the rush of being
In the tumultuous sound.

Power speaks with accent certain!
Force quickens in that wild roar!
An aeon lifts its curtain—
A billow crashes ashore.

SONNET OF PUNIC PEOPLES

O lady by proud Utica's dim sea,
What lovers brought their gifts where you
   should lie—
Queenly in many-gemmed sarcophagi—
Until an alien race found out the key?
Where rounded breasts of yours were regally
Adorned with amulets and scarabed gold,
What mourners brought a shimmering shroud,
   which told
An ancient faith of immortality?

These later breeds of men that desecrate
Your tombs without a qualm or thought of fear,
Who gave them mandate over seal and rite?
An hundred centuries hence, a requiting fate
Shall rob their own immortals in their bier,
And pen the tale of Time's unresting flight.

SPEAK TO ME

I love the hills my Saviour trod,
The vales where He communed with God,
Jerusalem, where blossoms sweet
And palm leaves carpeted the street.

As Thou didst speak at Pentecost,
O Jesus, speak to me or chide;
But speak to me, with me abide,
Speak, speak to me!

It cannot be that Thou art lost,
Thy Father's house lies never far;
Thy promises still with us are,
And time was only younger when,

My Saviour, Thou wert here with men,
And space, 'tis just as wide as then—
Thou mayest surely come again,
Speak, speak to me!

O Love of mine transmute,
This love I bear for earth,
And give it Heavenly birth!
Hang Thou about it now
A halo from Thy brow—
O speak to me!

Make sacred my desire,
And set my soul afire
With love of Thee!
Bend down Thy kingly head,
That impress of the thorns I see,
And speak to me!
Reach out Thy hands that bleed,
For Thee I sorely need—
O speak to me!

Jesus, my Saviour, mine!
Speak Thou tonight,
Illumine with Thy light,
My hope! my love! my God!
Hear Thou my vow,
O let me now
Thy vision see,
Speak—speak to me!

SWORDS

They flash and lunge and grimly thrust,
  Their slithering sharpness pierces me,—
But my resistance is as dust
  Against the onslaught of the sea.

The sword of Damocles hangs low
  As up I look with wondering air;
The Samurai could plunge it so,
  With damask touch across the hair.

The sword of Solomon defends,
  Baring my inmost urge to err—
As Knights once fought with Saracens,
  And drew for Holy Sepulchre.

Saint Peter's blade leaps forth for me,
  And only Christ discerns his thought:
Herodias would gladly see
  My head upon a charger brought.

All these! And have I struck in turn,
  Caring no whit for Christ, my Lord?
Whose sword for blood doth redly yearn,
  Must perish by the selfsame sword!

THE PRISONER

Beauty is imprisoned in girlish flesh,
  And, struggling to escape its bonds, must fail.
It is caparisoned in rich battle-mail
  That holds the living spirit in a mesh.

Beauty cannot escape its carnate place
  Except by age, or fear, or ravishing.
All these can set the fluttering dove a-wing,—
  Then whither may it fly in starry space?

THE OCEAN BURIAL

Bury in cold and chilly earth
Unfeeling, chilly hearts.
To that embrace let them return
From out the crowded marts
Of cities, lost to joyous mirth.

But one young, gentle and refined
Whose clay must lie at rest,
For such fair temple let us find
A place in ocean's breast,
And bid her lie where waves are kind.

It is not well that fair and lovely forms
Should rest where foul destructions blindly
      creep—
Beneath the callous earth at last
That lissome, rounded limbs find sodden sleep.
Dead shells on ocean's bed are safe from storms!

Then place her there, and shed no tears,
Where wave the tinted arms of weeds
With nacreous hands and rainbow eyes.
Oh, leave her there beneath the reeds
That rise and fall through days and years!

The glow of pearls close by her head,
The trailing weed a winding sheet,
Where colored fishes softly kiss
And tufty moss upholds her feet,
Where ocean flowers adorn the dead!

THE MASTER EARTH

It lies there coarse and sprawling
    Where God flung it down to its fate,
A Gargantuan live thing
    Of lust and love and hate.

Its hairy limbs are mountains,
    Its breast the valleys below,
Its passion swells in fountains
    That run and race and flow.

The sea is a clinging woman
    Who glides to her lover's breast,—
A desire-exhausted woman
    Who lies on the earth to rest.

The earth is brutal and spurns her;
    Weeds she wears who was bride.
Sobbing and crying, she turns her
    Wet face to the ebbing tide.

I said: "The sea is weeping—
    It steals from its master's shore."
Then I saw the water creeping
    To the earth's embrace once more.

THE MOON MESSAGE

High over the feathery tree tops
   Rides the moon in mystery white,
And below, the murmuring river
   Mirrors her delicate light.

Away on the cold, tall mountains
   Shines a dazzling cap of snow,
While the moon sends earth a message
   That illumines the river's flow.

"Roll on, O earth, my brother!
   Panoramic, majestic your robe.
Highlands and valleys and cities
   Are gemmed in your swinging globe.

"I behold your seas and sway them,
   I send you reflected light;
The stars and Pleiades wonder—
   My eclipse is dark like the night.

"Once I was rock of your roughness,
   Once I was ring of your crust;
But now I am your brother,
   Traversing the bright star-dust."

MUSIC

Unveiled hast thou another sphere,
And over seas of azure clear,
On wings, now slow, now subtly fleet,
Thou com'st, and ah! my pulses beat
To rhythmic sounds unknown before;
My feet press hard upon the shore
Of wide and silvery, shining sea,
Across whose waves thou callest me.

And then, with notes that ever rise,
Thy martial tones assail the skies
And, sinking once again all low,
Thy subtle strain grows soft and slow.
I feel its meaning, almost seize,
And so implore, on bended knees,
That thou wilt make thy raptures clear,
That thou wilt bring thy sirens near.

But, as I grasp at joys unknown,
New beauties flash, the others flown;
Faster they come, I hold my breath
Lest silvery sounds so sweet mean death.

This, Music, is thy shining sea,
Whose gentle waves roll in to me,
With sounds too sweet for mortal ear,
With notes too dear for man to hear.

Upon this shore of thine I stand
And, longing, look for unseen strand,
Whose verge is fair and far away,
Unfathomed save by passion's ray.

I'll leave the stolid world behind
And launch my bark, that shore to find!

THE LOVE SONGS OF TOMORROW

What will they be,
  Love songs of tomorrow?
How youth sings to youth
  Tells joy and sorrow?

Will they be Pagan, sensuous songs
  Of riotous blood and wanton eyes?
Will they seize an immemorial earth
  And miss the gates of Paradise?

I think I see Him coming, singing
  Down old Jerusalem's highway—
Is this tomorrow's gentle Lover
  Whose songs of love sound faint today?

THE HILLMAN

Happiness was springing in him,
  The preacher men came to see:
It was said he cleansed a leper
  By the main road at Bethany.

They followed him from villages,
  From seashore and upland-farms,—
And spread their coats and garments down,
  With branches, gathered in their arms.

Joyously he received their praises,
  And smiled upon the greening holt:
They shouted when they saw him mounting,
  Bareback on the unbroken colt.

More he seemed than simply human,
  There in Mount Olive's welcome shade;
Then he rode away to Calvary,
  Gentle, helpful, unafraid.

GODHEAD

Not the lights of the city but the light of the
　　stars,
Nor the light of the stars but the light of love—
　The light that is clearer than reddening Mars,
The dawn from spiritual spheres above.

Not the sounds of the night but beyond all
　　sound,
Nor the sights of the day but further than sight—
　From the outermost space where havens
　　abound,
From the spiritual manger of mystic light.

Yes, purer than spirits, more hallowed than
　　they,
Glorified, rarefied, beyond their ken—
　Of the total of perfectness in every vast way,
Are the impulses of Godhead that come unto
　　men.

LEGEND OF A CUP OF COLD WATER

Sing the tale of the Christ Child!
A drama of ages ago,
How Bethlehem bled for its glory,
And Nazareth dared the foe;
How Herod sent out his soldiers,
Brutal and base and wild,
To take the lives of the children—
And innocence was defiled.

On to the land of Egypt
A Father and Mother fled,
With the Child that men called Jesus,
A price on His princely head.
Near to the vale of Jordan,
But half along their way,
Joseph and Mary were fainting
In the dust and heat of the day,
When down from the hills rode soldiers
With blood of babes on their swords—
Red gold was paid by Herod
To all his hireling hordes.

And quick to his galley marching,
A Roman drove his slaves,
Prodded and beaten and parching,
Athirst for the cup that saves.
In purple and jeweled baubles
The Palatine rode his steed

And they met, in that sun-scorched valley,
The soldiers aflame with greed.
And there, by a shepherd's stable,
Stood Mary and Jesus the Child,
And there, on that angry babel,
He looked, compassionate, mild.
He gazed on Roman and soldier
And heard the clash of blade,
And a manacled captive lifted
His bleeding hands for aid.
And Jesus, the infant Saviour,
Went down midst that brutal band,
And lo, a cup of cold water
He held in His baby hand.

And a stillness came over the babel
And the cruel blows were stayed
And Mary, there by the stable,
And Joseph were unafraid.
Then hastened the Chief to his galley
And the soldiers rode rough-shod
And left in peace in that valley
Jesus, the Prince of God.

FROM ROSE LAND

I loved men's roses as a nun
              Loves roses.
Red blossoms stirred my life! The sun
   Oft burned them till the petals bled;
   But youth was like a bridal bed,
   While far ahead the specters fled.

A rover's gift from Arab hands!
              Gold roses.
We traveled far by desert sands,—
   Went winding on to Nedjed bold,
   Where roses grew of Ophir gold,
   And old love tales were nightly told.

A Venice merchant gave my lips
              Pink roses;
On to Cathay we went in ships
   That fetched young girls from China's shore,
   And jars of rose leaves packed in store,—
   Leaves more like weavings from Lahore.

I walked in gardens of delight,—
              Life's roses.
There revelry prevailed by night,
   But it has blanched my face to gray;
   Torn rose leaves strew my path today,
   To hurt my soul and bid me pray.

As sorrow scans the backward years,
   White roses,
Dank with the dew of futile tears—
 White roses like lost joys—I see.
 Thorns crucify the heart of me
 On Calvary—Love's Calvary.

ESCAPING

I day-dreamed that I was pursued,
That I escaped the pursuing officers,
That I outgeneraled them,
Or, with heroic daring, excelled them;
And then I drifted down across the border
Of a neighboring country,
There to re-establish my prestige,
Compel recognition
And vindicate my innocence.

But now I have found another borderline—
An unsuspected rendezvous
In a newly-envisioned state.
I can go at will,
In the twinkling of an eye,
And no pursuing officer can arrest my flight.
The country is near at hand.

From my pillow or my armchair,
Or the crowded elbowing street
I can take my way at will.
Love is my passport,
Awakened understanding my guide,
And often dear ones, gone before,
Whisper to me or send messages
By God's sweet grace,
Yes, I will vindicate my standpoint
Over there—

Immortality!   Service!
The whole universe
A spiritual proposition,
Love the motive and the goal.

DEPRESSION

The city roared at my casement,
   The city throbbed to my heart,
Dragon-like from its caverns,
   Tumultuous from its mart.

And I at my lofty window
   Leaned to the shivering night
And knew the hell and misery
   And the bitter cold and fright.

Wearily looked I upward
   To the appealing, star-gemmed sky,
And wondered if God's mercy
   Were true or yet but a lie.

IF SHE WOULD COME BACK

If she would come back now, in the flesh I mean,
    And walk beside me as once she calmly
        walked,
I would be good to her nor yet demean
    Myself with selfishness that closely stalked

By my right hand—Oh, if she would return
    And put upon me mighty deeds to do,
How gladly I would bend my soul to earn
    The fulfillment of her desires, her wishes new.

If she would come back, bid me lead the fight
    For her or for any cause she had espoused,
God knows I'd be a hero and never flight
    Should dim the valiant flame she had aroused.

If she would come back and bid me patient be,
    Love her own people as I worshiped mine,—
(Hold! who wrote those strange words, who
        made so free?)
    Yes, God—I hear, her will and also Thine.

If she would come back—

THE TOURMALINE

The lapidary with glistening stones
Sets three a-row, his trinity.
Red ruby—Christ, Thy blood atones!
White diamond—Mary's virginity!

But red is, too, a passionate breast
With lust and power and anger rife.
The diamond speaks of supernal rest,—
The ruby throbs with strong, hot life.

Then lovingly comes the tourmaline,
Soft lavender suffused with rose.
Part flesh part spirit, in its sheen,
The glory of gentle tolerance glows.

MY HOUSE OF PRAYER

It stands close by the climbing road,
  My mystic house with gardens fair;
'Tis window-bright, this glad abode—
  I take my hopes, my longings there.

Its aura is of flowering brush:
  The pungent perfume wafts to me;
It sweetly comes in twilight's hush
  When purpling skies glow rapturously.

My house of prayer is sculpture-graced,
  Deep music echoes down its halls,
Rich paintings lean, like women laced,
  And books are high along its walls.

On that warm hearth doth peace descend.
  My house with wide and lordly stair
Hath majesties that glory lend,—
  And this I know: God answers prayer.

OLD SHOES

Old shoes are cryptic things on human feet—
They press along a way that's hard or sweet.
  I see them go from London down to Kew,—
  And some are shoes that danced the gay night
    through.

Oh, how alike old shoes are to our hearts!
Mayhap a beggar we, a queen with tarts;
  But we must go, there is no place to rest—
  Old shoes, worn out? God take us to His
    breast!

OLD JOYS

Old joys, messieurs, are grievous things
   That haunt the heart and change to pain—
They float upon a viol's strings
   Or in a woman's voice again.

Old joys are like a cruel jest—
   I feel your upturned face and breath:
God ease my heart that stirred your breast
   And grant to me a welcome death.

Or stay! be this my better prayer—
   Let me, inspired, serve needy men:
Perchance I'll hear you in the air,
   Whispering courage to me then.

POET'S MEED

And while the poet with his bleeding side
Makes others bleed,
What has he done?
What meed
Is his by law
Of men?
To hope
And then,
A little clapping of the hands,
A little glow from setting sun,
A flower or two for race that's run.

But when a tender child
Or weary soul
Shall see those lines
And find them white as snow
And not all red,
And by them lifted up shall be
And made more strong,
What then, I say, is poet's meed?
Behold the law and sweetly read
That when a star the weak shall see,
That star shines brightly unto Me.

STAR CALLED

Oh, a young lad, a noble lad, a chorister to Him,
Was called away but yesterday to starry regions
     dim!

He was my own, my own dear boy and I am very
     sad;
But one is free in telling me to be a little glad.

For Death's a friend and not the end, though still
     a mighty hewer,—
For a young boy, a virgin boy, we are forever
     sure.

His soul will fly up there on high and to some
     waiting star,
For never vileness has he known nor anything to
     mar.

Oh, a young lad, a sweet, dear lad, and a chorister
     then,
Was called away on yesterday but I shall smile
     again!

PICTURES AND PROSPECT

I will return to other, happier days,
  I will escape my dull imprisonment,—
Appease the hungry heart that fiercely says:
  Give back the careless years that boyhood
    spent!

Three vanished, happy pictures beckon me:
  A chattering wren upon a bush of sage,
The southern sun, and I full wantonly
  Go wandering forth in boyhood's knightly
    age.

O silent dawn, gray-turbaned, mystic dawn
  As we awoke about our cold camp-fire!
Ah, outing times and rendezvous now gone;
  When I loved best my dashing horseman-sire!

A nautilus upon the Gulfweed Sea,
  And only argosies would give it chase;
A man-o-war, a pink-sailed Portugee
  That jauntily won the wrack-entangled race.

O candled age! If you have aught to excell
  These pictured scenes that show my youth's
    heyday,
Then fain would I forego my boyhood's spell
  And fare me out on life's amazing way.

RACE MEMORY

You siren, brown-eyed and savage,
  With wind-blown, fragrant hair,
I loved you with love primeval
  When you were not woman nor fair.
As we roamed in the mountain fastness
  Ten thousand years ago,
I was your lord and lover,
  And brought you a bleeding doe.

That tawny strand in my fingers,
  As I stroke your hair away,
Brings thought of a one-time nearness
  As you drowsed and beside me lay
In old days on the Euphrates,
  In the Asian jungle deep,—
When you were a mate and mother
  In a tiger's love-tamed sleep.

Do you remember, sweetheart,
  When the king from Babylon
Rode out with his spear-armed hunters,
  And the sport had just begun?
You were hurt. Your eyes blazed fiercely,
  And I sprang with the force of rage
High up on the elephant's shoulders,
  To the purple riding cage.

There the king of Babylonia
    I crushed and tore apart,
Before his hunters could kill me
    With their spears red in my heart.

SEEING CARCASSONNE

I rode by sage and laurel on the hill
And best of all the scented, jade-green bey;
  Upon a sunny mesa found poppies fill
The vision as amorous sunlight fills the day.

  Eager, all mood, oblivious of limbs and feet,
I paused and climbed up to that holy height,
  Where angel and thunderbird will often
      meet,—
The stars pierced through me all that glittering
      night.

WHAT A LITTLE CHILD CAN DO

The strange mutations of the world
Had bred within my bosom hate:
Defeat its crushing bludgeons hurled;
I cared no more for love's estate,
Nor heeded faces at my gate.
And then within the crowded street
I heard the story of the East,—
Of children wanting bread to eat,
While every day I sat at feast.
My hoarded gold I brought that night,
In our own Christ Child's very name:
They told me hunger's sobbing plight
Would find relief, with want and shame,—
And love sprang in my heart aflame!

THE PRAYER OF GLOOM

Aimlessly wandering at dawn of day,
Unknowing I strayed from the beaten way,
Where men go to and fro,
Till halting at last at a lonely spot,
Away from my God and by men forgot,
My head I bended low.

I was young, but the years oppressed,
I was weary, my woe confessed;
Nature was blank, and Love was a lie;
I sank on the earth and the welcome tears
Refused to come, nor devilish fears
To rouse me more as the time went by.

How long I may not tell
Mine eyes stared into Hell,
When onward flowed a cloud
My ghastly gaze to shade,
Came dark and dripping to my aid
And threatened me, as a shroud.

I prayed this hovering Gloom to lower
And cover me with grave clothes o'er;
Mine arms stretched I aloft,
As came the stormy wraith,
Drawn by my mighty faith,
And spilled its rain-drops soft.

Then raged the gale,
On frail earth,—frail;
In awe I held my breath.
Bent were the trees,
Blown to their knees—
They menaced me with death.

THE PAGAN BEYOND

What is the thing that love is called?
That bends the being to its will,
That gives the soul its wildest thrill,
Defies a God and dares a hell
And makes a man his birthright sell
Because a woman has enthralled.

What is the thing of life most fair?
That makes the sweets of striving pall,
That is itself one thing and all,
That is of honor its own code,
That tramples others in the road
And tears the heart and lays it bare.

Is there at last, beyond, above,
A reason for this wild desire,
A siren who has set on fire
The blood in throbbing heart?
A woman of consummate art
Who captivates through perfect love.

MARY AND JESUS AND JEANNE

When lands my ship of soul upon a shore
  Whose light is luminous and spirit-made,
And I shall count my longings o'er and o'er
  And look with hope upon each passing shade,
    There will be three
    That I shall want to see—
Jesus, the Christ, whom I have learned to love,
  Mary who held him and led him by the hand,
And Jeanne d'Arc who wore a warrior's glove
  And dared her martyred way to spirit-land.

    While yet I find
    My own earth-friends and kind,
These three I'll seek: the One who took man's
      part
And served His way to every broken heart,
  And Mary, Virgin Mother of Bethlehem:
  Like the wise men I shall joyfully worship
    them.
    And her I'll see,
    The girl of Domremy,
Jeanne d'Arc, the second child that came,
Sister to Jesus but unknown to Jesus' fame,
  Reborn in later centuries to love and fight—
  These three I'll seek when ship of mine takes
    flight.

A POSSIBILITY

Satiety ruled the earth
When, like a bolt from Heaven,
There came a ship from out the blue.
No Viking drove it
But a being like a woman
Had command.
She was fair and slender and ethereal
And her crew were like unto her.
They could not speak or write and seldom
       smiled:
Their language was flashed from eye to eye.
Their ship was silvery metal—
Proud it looked
And sucked the air with a pleasing sound.
Speaking and communication
Were not possible—
Then some one brought a chart of the heavens:
The visitor from out the sky
Put down her finger on the planet Mars.

THE EARTH-SOUL

The earth has a soul,
  O ye people!
    Cry it forth with the bells
  In the steeple,
From the pole to the pole,
      To the many and few!
      The earth has a soul like you.

The earth has a soul,—aye, surely.
  It is conscious, knows love and hate;
It glows with feeling purely,
  And it bears the bludgeons of fate.
    It is ravished with love, impassioned;
      It yearns to change its swing
    In the great perihelion God fashioned,
      Where time is a little thing.
        Aye, soul there is in the planet,
          But mighty law prevails—
        Imprisoned in clay and granite,
          It feels the ceaseless gales
            Of space, the stress of heat and
              cold,
            The thunder of the beating surf,
        And all the friction of giant things.
            Yet, through it quick the turf
Grows green, the flowers unfold
        And, after every dawn, like jewels lies
          the dew

Which falls to swell the crystal springs;—
Yes, the earth has a soul like you.

I dreamed on the earth enraptured.
  I felt her warm embrace;
My gaze was heaven-captured,
  And the stars shone down on my face.
    I felt in my soul the earth-soul,—
      It was strong like the wind that blew,—
    And I knew in the night the earth-goal
      Of a breast that was jeweled with dew.
        Then the fingers of earth caressed me,—
          The trees and the flowers and grass;
            But her tears ran down with the
              torrent
          For the evil of men, alas.
            Ah, the earth has a soul,
              My people.
            Can you bring your soul into beat
              With the rhythm and throb of the
                earth-soul,
            There at the great God's feet?

VISION

Last night I saw a spirit form,
  It came and held its hands to me;
My heart and soul were like a storm
  That strove with wild expectancy.

A thousand doubts were solved that hour,
  A life-time's learning put to shame;
I'd rather have that spirit dower
  Than hoards of rubies all aflame.

Last night I saw my spirit bride
  Who'd flown like Autumn's swirling leaf;
She could not even in Heaven abide
  Except she come to cure my grief.

RETURN

They said that she was dead,
  And yet they had not put her down beneath
      the sod,
    With flowers and tears and last good-byes,
      Because she came as I was lying in a
          grove of trees.
They said that she was dead
  And yet, with fleeting glance and nod,
    I saw her hasten by with greeting in her
        eyes,
      Within the space that I could gain my
          knees.

They said that she was gone,
  And yet, last night, I read
    An old, half mystic tale
      Of how departed souls had sent a message
          back to earth.
They said that she was gone,
  And yet my thought was led
    To pause and, as I lowered the book, my
        face turned pale,
      For in my secret soul I felt rebirth.

You may not kill the Gods!
  The Gods return to broken pillars, fallen urns,
    Although our homage is no longer theirs—
      Although we worship with another face.

You cannot kill the Gods!
   Then why shall not the dear departed one, who
       yearns
      For human ties, come back adown those
         stairs
         That love has lit, and pause within her
           old accustomed place?

TRAVEL AND NATURE
POEMS

GO DOWN TO THE SEA

Go with the seagull down to the South Seas,
  Go with the molly hawk, the wild albatross;
A dark girl is praying down on her bare knees
  For me to come back to the warm Southern
    Cross.

I can see the white combers roll in from Aus-
    tralia
  To the sand-beautied beach where we had our
    palm shack;
Roll in from Java and Bali and Asia
  As if they were paying a tribute we lack.

My bride was a Princess, her father a Chieftain,
  He dowered us with tapa and rubies and rum;
But loving is changeful yet sometimes you'll win
  When death's at your side and the boom of a
    drum.

Go down with the steamer, the white ships a-
    sailing,
  Tahiti and Tonga and Fiji are there;
Old passions are crying and sea birds are wailing
  And life flaunts your face with magic and dare.

NUKA HIVA- E KAOHA

On your high bold cliffs Marquesas
Shines the glinting westing sun
And the sea birds circle upward, as
We sail, our visit done.

Nuka Hiva- E Kaoha,
We have seen Hesperides!
In a farewell like Aloha
Call we now across the seas:
Nuka Hiva- E Kaoha!

WE CAME SINGING TO TAHITI

We came singing, rapturously singing,
To Tahiti Island singing:
E Maururu a-vau.

Never from far Northland winging
Came there yet a message flinging:
Te Tiare Vare- au.

From a mighty white ship bringing
Brotherhood and good will now,
E Maururu a-vau.

We came giving, yes, forgiving
Every frown upon a brow,
Te Tiare Vare- au.

Mist clouds on high mountains clinging,
We must follow our ship's prow,
E Maururu a-vau.

We came singing, brothers singing,
Sweethearts have received our vow:
Te Tiare Vare- au.

Note—This poem embodies the Tahitian National Anthem, which
means: I love you. How do you do? My love for you is like the
scented lotus.

SOUTH SEA TRAGEDY

My Lady in a distant city,
  You know that Fijian day
  When we went from the immaculate steamer,
  There in the coral bay,—
  You were an Aphrodite
  In your shimmering tropic gown
  And I was your Pan, your dreamer,
  As the blazing sun went down.

We found a cornucopia,
  A kelea shell that spoke,—
  Oh, the spell of Viti Levu
  And the brown chiefs and their folk!
  I was drunk with native kava
  And knew not the things I said
  And I lost my pure-lipped Lady,—
  I took me a brown girl to wed.

When the ships come to ancient Suva
  I see through a forest crack,—
  How I hate you yet love you, Suva!
  For I never can go back.

FAIR TREACHEROUS CORAL REEFS

Fair treacherous South Sea coral reefs,—
God placed them out safeguarded miles
   Around each palm-green tropic strand
And through them gateways, doors bewhiles,
   That harbouring ships might come to land.

They are I think like island chiefs,—
To know them well is safe for me;
   To know them ill a danger sure.
We saw a wreck, a tragedy
   That coral struck nor would endure.

The breakers clashed like men's beliefs
Against those wrecks on coral reefs.

LOVE IN SOUTHERN SEA

Man whose way with maid hath been,
Through years of happy longing,
To taste her sweets and seek again,
Unsatisfied in wronging;
Whose amorous arms have ever known
Beauty fair but quickly flown,—
Go to isle in Southern sea,—
There a brown maid waiteth thee.

THE STARS AND STRIPES AT PAGO PAGO

Then hail the silken Stripes and Stars
   That welcome me and you,—
I saw it wave o'er Pago spars,
   The Stripes, the Stars and Blue.

I saw the bare Samoan men
   In that South Sea Island town
And something in my heart spoke then
   For my brother though he be brown.

The Flag, the Flag, Emblem of Right,
   Far down through the South Sea gates,—
There are banners sullied, but ours is bright,
   The Flag of the United States.

IN HONOLULU

We were docked in Honolulu,—
  In a palm-thatched home were guests,
And the oil lamps smoked and sputtered
  On the hula dancers' breasts.

Oh, your brown bare limbs, Eloha!
  Still they curve and kiss and yearn,
With the hair about your shoulders,
  And about your waist the fern!

Our brave captain's eyes looked guileless;
  She was sweet, ah, yes! But, hark!
Quick we whisper, then we struggle
  As we drag him to our barque.

Fare you well, brown girl, Eloha!
  Lithe Eloha, fare you well!
When a sailor loves a brown girl,
  They must part. Oh, long farewell!

FROM HAWAII TO THE
GOLDEN GATE

We saw ahead the Golden Gate.
  Majestically the dawn o'ertopped
  The mountains, and blue night was stopped.
Then came the sun like brilliant fate.

That orb had shone on slumbering Greece,
  The Golden Horn and ancient Rome.
  Its light had struck the mighty dome
Of Peter's, made the star-shine cease.

On, on it came where ocean flows,
  Columbus-like it sought West lands,—
  Great Washington's white shaft withstands
Its light awhile, then radiant glows.

The sun outstrips the prairie lands,
  The covered van to airship high,—
  It dowers the Golden Gate and nigh
Are we with leis from brown love-hands.

HAVANA

Along the Prado walked a young mother
In Havana.
She led a little girl-child
Adorned in barbaric splendor,
With a tassel pendant from her lustrous hair.

The orange-red scarf
Thrown across the dimpled shoulders
Fell barely below the armpits.
A golden neck-piece
High about the throat
Uptilted the tiny pagan face.

No more than this the resplendent muchacha
        wore.

She smiled at me in unfathomable abandon,
Sheer and pure and sweet,
And I, enthralled,
Gave back an answering smile.

It was the Spirit of the Prado
Which I beheld!

THE SANTA CECILIA PARROT

Parrot or cockatoo or bird
  Of happy omen and rare,—
Oh, will you give ear to my word?
  You should be more debonnaire.

You funny, comma-billed bird,
  Red-feathered and blue and green,
When I was gloriously young I heard
  Your call, hoarse, guttural and keen.

Today you cry mockingly, and screech;
  While the old chanties of the sea
And brown girls, moonlight and sea beach
  Come back, heart-hauntingly, to me.

THE ROCKS OF RAMIREZ

Long years ago with childish eyes
I gazed upon a mountain grand,
That reached its dazzling, hoary height
Up, up into the azure skies.
I wondered then in childish spell
How many years were passed and gone
Since first that lordly mountain rose,
Or first the waters from it fell
And left it there in grim repose.

In later days I roved the seas
And once away to southward sailed,
Where, rounding ice-bound, wild Cape Horn,
I saw the rocks of Ramirez.
They jut, an island, through the blue
And billowy, storm-wracked, salty waves,
Defying all that ever sail,
Diego Ramirez,—but you,
And sea and sky and south wind's wail!

Against those crags the billows dashed,
The white spray stung their beetling cliffs,
The sea birds circled round the shores,
With sullen roars the ocean crashed.
I see it still, the salt sea foam,
Climb up the lichened sides to fall!
We passed the rocks of Ramirez

And set our yearning sails for home;
But memory yet is on the seas.

Note—The author, when a boy, sailed around Cape Horn on an English merchantman bound from San Pedro, California, to Queenstown, Ireland. He uses the word Ramirez as the sailors pronounced it,—accent on the last syllable (rez).

THE DOGS OF NIAGARA

Unleashed, the billows run
   Throwing the waters back;
They leap and snap in fun,
   They snarl and spurn the track.

A thousand dogs come on,
   Shaking their frothy lips,
Charging where men have gone
   Down with their broken ships.

On with a leap and roar
   To the perilous edge of doom,
On through Niagara's door,
   Where the waters roar and boom,—

Over the brink to the hell
   Of that mist-choked gorge they're gone,—
Dead in a fate most fell!—
   But Niagara still sweeps on.

THE GREAT TEMPLE AND THE GREATER LOVE

Fair shines the moon upon the Taj,
The fronded palms wave fair
And on thy coral strand, Mahal,
The rose clouds kiss the air.

Through Agra's old palatial streets
There hurries now the seneschal
To spread his rich barbaric feast
In honor of the prized Mahal.

But temples crumble, cities die
And feasting hours are past—
Yet love that's lighter than a sigh
Endures until the last.

THE FATED RHINE

Down from a thousand mountain heights
   Leap streams of melted snow,
And, from fair vales of blue and green,
   The mist clouds upward go.

A thousand bubbling, crystal springs
   Give out their life-draught still
And, sweeping o'er the German plains,
   The storm king stoops to fill

The banks of ancient, storied Rhine;
   While up the Northern main
The whistling, bold winds wilder blow,
   With skirts of driving rain.

But more there is to fated Rhine:
   Her waters run with tears
That love and hate and strife have shed,
   While war spelled out the years.

Where Frank and Gaul have lived and loved
   And drunk life's cup of wine,
Sword thrust and bursting cannon ball
   Make red the fated Rhine.

BYRD AT THE POLE

Mighty the treacherous ice about the peaks,
   Beyond the Spitzbergen, beyond the seas.
The wild birds in the air have striking beaks,—
   They wing the utmost North with daring ease.

Perhaps the tropics were exchanged for this—
   Who knows but time, and time's old buc-
      caneers?
But if a naked maiden gave her kiss,
   It was long ages since, a million years.

Cold staring eyes look on the snow and ice
   And glaciers move, insistent in their pace—
They grip the awful mountains like a vice
   And birds and seals behold no human face.

Then comes a hero from the Bay of Kings!
   A fiery angel could no stranger be
Than his wide ship with sky-hung, questing
      wings
   That settles there in daring majesty.

An Arctic flight, supreme in earth's long age!
   And he has hurtled to the mystic Pole—
The Gods reveal a scintillating page,
   They cannot play a more undying role.